Little Victori

A play

Shaun Prendergast

Samuel French — London
New York - Toronto - Hollywood

© 1994 by SHAUN PRENDERGAST

Rights of Performance by Amateurs are controlled by Samuel French Ltd, 52 Fitzroy Street, London W1P 6JR, and they, or their authorized agents, issue licences to amateurs on payment of a fee. **It is an infringement of the Copyright to give any performance or public reading of the play before the fee has been paid and the licence issued.**

The Royalty Fee indicated below is subject to contract and subject to variation at the sole discretion of Samuel French Ltd.

Basic fee for each and every
    performance by amateurs   Code J
in the British Isles

The Professional Rights in this play are controlled by MICHELINE STEINBERG, 110 Frognal, London NW3 6XU

The publication of this play does not imply that it is necessarily available for performance by amateurs or professionals, either in the British Isles or Overseas. Amateurs and professionals considering a production are strongly advised in their own interests to apply to the appropriate agents for consent before starting rehearsals or booking a theatre or hall.

ISBN 0 573 05103 8

Please see page iv for further copyright information

LITTLE VICTORIES

First presented at the Queen Elizabeth Hall, London as a co-production between Trestle Theatre Company and Quicksilver Theatre for Children on 11th January 1994 with the following cast:

Tony	Damien Shaw
Josie	Debi Mastel
Debs	Anna Carus-Wilson
Gordon	Alan Riley

All other parts played by members of the company

Directed by Graham Walters and Toby Wilsher
Designed by Mark Wilsher
Lighting by Leslie Phillip Shaw and Jo Joelson
Music by Sally Cook

COPYRIGHT INFORMATION

(See also page ii)

This play is fully protected under the Copyright Laws of the British Commonwealth of Nations, the United States of America and all countries of the Berne and Universal Copyright Conventions.

All rights including Stage, Motion Picture, Radio, Television, Public Reading, and Translation into Foreign Languages, are strictly reserved.

No part of this publication may lawfully be reproduced in ANY form or by any means—photocopying, typescript, recording (including video-recording), manuscript, electronic, mechanical, or otherwise—or be transmitted or stored in a retrieval system, without prior permission.

Licences for amateur performances are issued subject to the understanding that it shall be made clear in all advertising matter that the audience will witness an amateur performance; that the names of the authors of the plays shall be included on all programmes; and that the integrity of the authors' work will be preserved.

The Royalty Fee is subject to contract and subject to variation at the sole discretion of Samuel French Ltd.

In Theatres or Halls seating Four Hundred or more the fee will be subject to negotiation.

In Territories Overseas the fee quoted above may not apply. A fee will be quoted on application to our local authorized agent, or if there is no such agent, on application to Samuel French Ltd, London.

VIDEO-RECORDING OF AMATEUR PRODUCTIONS

Please note that the copyright laws governing video-recording are extremely complex and that it should not be assumed that any play may be video-recorded for whatever purpose without first obtaining the permission of the appropriate agents. The fact that a play is published by Samuel French Ltd does not indicate that video rights are available or that Samuel French Ltd controls such rights.

CHARACTERS

Tony
Josie, his friend
Debs, Tony's mother
Gordon, Debs's boyfriend (non-speaking, fully masked)

Josie's mother (fully masked)
Josie's doctor (fully masked)
Sumo baby Josie

Chorus of dogs (half-masked)
Sniffer dog
Gendarme dog

The dogs play the following non-speaking roles:
French waiter
French policemen

Production note: The dogs are half-masked and only speak ad lib gibberish, unless they are speaking in French, which they do fluently, or singing. TV, film and music references can be updated if desired. Most of the special effects can be performed by the cast.

To
John, Mary, Alison, Andrea,
Calum and Annie Rose

ACT I

A kitchen

The stage is in darkness

At the back of the auditorium floats a luminous moon. It moves towards the stage, pursued by an excited pack of dogs, who clamber through the audience. They try to reach it by standing on each others' shoulders and climbing on the back of the seats. When the moon reaches the centre of the stage, the dogs assume a tableau and begin to howl. It is a mournful sound, both a lamentation and a prayer. They begin to scamper about, then notice the audience for the first time. They react with low-pitched growls at first, then stalk forward aggressively. One of the dogs starts scratching itself, then others. A fight ensues. Two dogs exit and the remaining dogs sniff each others' backsides. They growl at the audience once more, then resume their howling at the moon. We hear a baby crying. The Lights snap up on Tony and Josie. Tony is holding a baby (puppet) in his arms, with its back to the audience. Josie runs towards the dogs, scaring them away

Josie Shoo, go on, get out of it! (*To the audience*) Don't worry about them ...
Tony Mangy things, making all that noise, they've woke the baby up. Go on, shoo. (*Mimicking Arnold Schwarzenegger*) "Hasta la vista, baby! Get out of it, eat my shorts!"

The baby cries

Josie (*to the baby*) Shh ...
Tony Not you baby. Them babies.
Josie Shut up and introduce us.
Tony (*to the audience*) OK, this is baby Josie.
Josie Named after me. I'm his friend.
Tony That's Josie, big Josie, instead of ...
Josie } (*together*) Little Josie.
Tony }
Josie Shhh, there's a good girl. She's gorgeous.
Tony And I'm Tony. This is my new baby sister. Well, she's not new, she's been around for a while, she'll be one soon.

Josie Is it a year since?
Tony A year. A whole year.
Josie You'll be a big girl soon, eh? Won't you?
Tony Yes, you'll be a big girl. (*To the audience*) Do you wanna see her, eh?
Do you wanna meet her?
Josie (*to the audience*) You won't scare her, will you?
Tony 'Cos you are quite scary to look at — all of you! (*He points to an adult member of the audience*) 'Specially him. (*He ad libs*) As long as you promise not to frighten her ... Promise ...? All right, this is my little sister.

The baby puppet is revealed for the first time. It yawns and looks quizzically at the audience

Tony See? This is the audience. Not a pretty sight, are they?
Josie Well introduce yourselves. Everybody whisper your name quietly.
Tony Say hallo, Josie.

The baby burps

She can't talk yet but she made a little sound.

The baby strains, grimaces and fills her nappy

Josie And she's made a little smell as well, haven't you Josie?
Tony Oh no.

The stench is overpowering. Josie mimes being sick into the sink

Oh dear! With any luck the bottom fairy will come and sprinkle some magic dust. Lots of it.
Josie You always make such a fuss.
Tony She needs changing.
Josie Well change her.
Tony I can't.
Josie Why not?
Tony I'm only eight. I'll have to get Mum to do it.
Josie Why not get Gordon to do it? He's her dad.
Tony Yeah, great idea. We'll get Gordon to do it. Where is he?
Josie He's mending the sink.

Josie reveals Gordon, who is under the kitchen sink attempting to unblock it. The audience cannot see his face

Tony Gordon! Hey Gordon! (*He kicks Gordon's feet to attract his attention*)

There is a loud crash as Gordon bumps his head

Gordon appears. He is a full mask character, a well-meaning man with a heart of gold, but uncoordinated. He is rather harassed at the moment

Josie exits

She needs changing. Red alert, red alert, thunder bums are go! Gordon! She has done her dirty, now you must do your duty. Five, four, three, two, one! Lift off!

Tony hands Gordon nappy changing items; talc, cream, etc. He throws a clean nappy and it lands on Gordon's head. Gordon looks unimpressed

Come on, she's your daughter.

Tony's mum, Deborah Mason, enters. It's raining outside, her mac is soaking and she looks tired and bedraggled. She is carrying eight carrier bags stuffed with food and disposable nappies

Debs (*snapping*) Tony! Did you wake the baby?
Tony No, she needs changing.
Debs Well don't just stand there, Gordon, get on with it. I've got to put the shopping away. (*She begins to put the shopping away into the kitchen cupboards*)

Gordon sighs heavily and accepts his responsibilities. He takes the baby from Tony

Wash your hands before you change her, mind.
Tony No, don't wash your hands!
Debs Stop mucking about Tony, he's covered in grease.
Tony (*winding Gordon up*) Don't do it Gordon, it's very dangerous, please!

Gordon is puzzled and alarmed

Debs Why not?
Tony He's undone the sink. If he tries to wash his hands by pouring water

from the taps it'll go down the plughole but the plughole isn't connected to the downward pipe so it'll go all over the floor and the floor will be really slippy and you'll be walking along carrying a big rubbish bag of smelly dirty nappies and you'll slip on the floor and fall and break your neck and you'll be dead and the police will come and they'll arrest Gordon and put him in jail——

Gordon doesn't like the sound of this

——in a big castle with a mask over his face like Hannibal the Cannibal— "A plate of fava beans and a nice bottle of Chianti"—and you'll be dead and he'll be in jail and there'll be no-one left to look after me and Josie and the council will come and take Josie into care and it'll be just like Charles Dickens, "Can I have some more sir", "No you cannot have some more", instead you'll be sold to an evil man with warts on his nose like a bunch of grapes, but then Toxic Avenger will come and put slime all over the man with the warty nose, slobber slobber slobber slobber and Josie will be saved——

Gordon, caught up in the story, goes to defend baby Josie

——and she'll be adopted by a rich couple who'll live in a huge mansion next to a great beach like *Baywatch*, all wiggle wiggle wiggle "Help I'm drowning", "Cute buns missy", and the rich people will be really nasty just like in the soaps, and they'll bring Josie up to be really snotty nosed and I'll be thrown out of the house on to the streets where I'll end up living in a cardboard box and begging, "Got any spare change please", and then I'll start taking drugs and I'll end up dead in the gutter and it'll all be Gordon's fault!

Gordon is horrified at this idea

Debs Well he better go and wash his hands upstairs then, hadn't he?

Gordon agrees with this and hurries off with the baby. Debs also exits

Tony (*to the audience*) Good old Gordon, gormless Gordon, I love winding him up. See, ever since my dad died my mum's had loads of different boyfriends. Like once right, this bloke at the squash club took her out, he was called Kevin. And he had a huge nose and a really silly voice. He talked like this, "Hallo little man, my name's Kevin." But he didn't last very long 'cos Mum said he had really bad breath, which is true, right. Steeeeench!

Then the next one was called Matthew, and he was really funny because he was one of those grown-ups who was really old but pretends to be really young. You know what I mean ? Like he'd say things like "Wicked" and "Bad", and you know fine well they haven't got a clue what they're talking about. So Matthew got the push and then she didn't see anybody for a while, and there was just me and her and it was great, this all happened about a year ago right? And then one day I came in from school ...

Debs enters in her dressing-gown; she's just washed her hair and put her make-up on

Tony listens to a Walkman

Debs Tony, Aunty Lucy is coming round tonight ... Tony, are you listening to me? (*She switches the Walkman off*)
Tony I've gone deaf. (*He takes the Walkman off and shouts*) I've gone deaf!
Debs (*loudly*) No you haven't!
Tony Stop being silly, Mum. Wassamatter?
Debs Aunty Lucy will be looking after you tonight.
Tony Why?
Debs I'm going out. She'll be here soon.
Tony Why are you wearing lipstick?
Debs Now I want you to behave for Aunty Lucy, you can watch telly and she's going to cook you your favourite pizza.
Tony I don't want pizza.
Debs Don't be silly, you love pizza.
Tony Has it got onions in?
Debs I'll have to hurry, he'll be here in a minute.
Tony 'Cos I don't like onions.
Debs But I'll be back by nine o'clock.
Tony I'm not eating it if it's got onions in.
Debs Yes all right, I'll make sure she takes all the onions out.
Tony Who's he?
Debs After you've had your tea you can watch TV till eight and then it's bedtime, OK?
Tony Who's he? Who's this He you're waiting for?
Debs Just a bloke.
Tony What's his name? (*To the audience*) She hates telling me their names, she always mumbles this bit.
Debs (*mumbling*) Gordon.
Tony Sorry, what was that?
Debs Gordon.

Tony Just a little bit louder if you don't mind?
Debs Gordon.
Tony Gordon? (*To the audience*) As soon as I heard that name I knew he'd be a plonker. I could sense it. And I was right. Even the dogs at the bottom of our street knew he was a plonker.

There is the sound of barking off stage. Gordon is chased on by one of the dogs we saw earlier. He is wearing a duffel coat over his shell suit and sandals with socks under them. He carries a present

Debs (*to the dog*) SHOO! SHOO! Get out! Go home!

Gordon starts to leave

Not you, Gordon. (*To the dog*) Shoo!

The dog exits

Tony. This is Gordon.
Tony Is this your new boyfriend?
Debs Well, we're going out together.
Tony I don't believe it! A duffel coat!

Gordon is dismayed by Tony's sarcasm

Debs You don't believe what?
Tony You're going out with him?
Debs What's wrong with him?
Tony He looks a total prat.
Debs Says who?
Tony Says me.

Gordon is in the middle, like a tennis umpire

Debs Yeah?
Tony Yeah!
Debs Is that right?
Tony That's right!
Debs Well luckily you're not going out with him.
Tony Yeah, lucky for me.

Gordon tries to sneak off but Debs hauls him back by the hood of his duffel coat

Debs Yeah, lucky for me too!

Tony I wouldn't be seen dead with him.

Debs (*whispering*) He's got a present for you.

Tony A present! (*He suddenly smiles and becomes effusive. He mimicks Cilla Black*) "Gordon hallo chuck, welcome to Blind Date, isn't he lovely, we're going to have a lorra lorra laughs, that's right love, sit down, take the weight off your present." (*He provides Gordon with a chair*)

Gordon sits down for a few seconds then gets up and wanders nervously around the kitchen. Everything he touches he breaks; handles come off cupboards, etc.

Debs Good lad. I'm just going to get changed.

Tony Oh no! What are you gonna wear?

Debs None of your business.

Tony Yes it is!

Debs exits. Josie enters from an obscure part of the set

(*Calling after Debs*) You might be walking down the street in some of your stupid clothes and my friends might see you!

Josie You haven't got any friends except me.

Tony Shut up you, I didn't even know you when all this happened.

Josie Your mum looks great.

Tony She looks terrible, she keeps wearing those skin-tight leggings and she's too old for them, I mean let's face it, she's twenty-six, she's ancient, she'll be getting her pension soon.

Josie Well how do you want her to dress?

Tony She should dress properly, like an old person. Isn't that right Gordon?

Gordon is fiddling with the kitchen window blind. At the mention of his name he gets a shock and lets go, causing the blind to furl with a clatter. During the following, he picks up the Walkman and begins listening to it

Josie What, with a hat that ties under her chin——

Tony —and sensible brown shoes——

Josie —and a big tweed coat smelling of ointment——

Tony —she could have one of them baskets on wheels—(*mimicking*) "My grandchildren are in New Zealand you know ..."

Josie and Tony sneak up to Gordon and turn the Walkman off. Gordon, thinking he's gone deaf, takes off the earphones and hits himself on the side of the head. Tony and Josie mime talking. Gordon gets really worried

(*Loudly*) Right, where's this present then, Gordon?

Gordon is shocked by Tony's loud voice. Tony snatches the present from Gordon's hands and looks at it disdainfully

What a mess.

Josie It looks very nice. If I'd known you were like this when I met you I'd never have hid under that table in France.

Tony Well honestly, it's bound to be rubbish! I mean a bloke in a duffel coat and sandals isn't going to give you a Nintendo, is he? This is going to be a smelly present I'll bet. Something like ... it's gonna be the *Ladybird Guide to Playing the Clarinet.* Or socks even. Yeah, he's the sort of bloke who thinks he can get on your good side with a box of Maltesers and a pair of socks.

Josie Well unwrap it then.

Tony unwraps the present. Light glows from it. There is thunder and lightning; intimations of the Death-Dealer world. Josie looks about in wonder. Tony's eyes remain fixed upon the present

Josie Tony, it's gone cold.

Tony It's ...

Josie There are shadows. I'm scared.

Bits of the room begin to transform into the Death-Dealer landscape. Images of a monstrous baby Josie appear and disappear from mundane places such as the microwave and the washing machine

I'm so cold. There's a cloud across the sky.

Tony (*still transfixed*) It's ...

Josie Look at Gordon!

The alphabetical fridge magnets move of their own accord to spell out "LIFE AND DEATH", and Gordon transforms into the Silent Wizard, who is part of the Death-Dealer game

What's happening? What is it?
Tony It's a DEATH-DEALER!
Josie Oh, is that all.

The kitchen, and Gordon, return to normal

Tony Wow! Death-Dealer, level one hundred.
Josie You dossy thing.
Tony Mega-wicked, this is the best one yet.
Josie You spawny rat.
Tony State of the art up to the minute grade one top level stuff?
Josie Well say thank you to Gordon.
Tony Who'd have thought that a prat like him would get me a Death-Dealer!
And if he buys me this on the first date what's he gonna buy me when she
kisses him for the first time? I mean, he'll have to give me a car or
something.
Josie He's waiting.
Tony And the first time he sleeps over? He'll have to buy me a house.
Josie You don't deserve friends, you! Serve you right if he doesn't give you
the other present!
Tony Another present? He must be rich! Perhaps he's one of them concentric
millionaires, what have got lots of money and don't know what to do with
it—(*to Gordon*) give it to me, give it to me, you are hypnotized, give it to
me concentric millionaire, 'cos they dress like tramps. It's true.

Gordon, hypnotized, falls to his knees

Right where's this other present?

Gordon searches on the ground

Come on, come on, I haven't got all day. What is it, a telly? A computer,
a compact disc player, a cuddly toy? What's on the board Miss Ford?

Gordon finds an envelope and hands it to Tony sheepishly

Our survey says ... uhn-uhn! An envelope?

*Debs enters dressed in a very glamorous frock. She looks like a million
dollars. Gordon wakes from hypnosis only to fall into another trance at the
sight of her*

Debs (*noticing the envelope*) Well open it.

Tony This had better be money!

Debs Tony!

Tony (*to Gordon*) Are you listening, gormless? 'Cos if this is a book token you can stick it up your duffel coat.

Debs Go on, open it.

Tony This is like the Oscars. And the winner is ... (*He opens the envelope*) Three tickets to Boe Lounge. Boe Lounge? What's a Boe Lounge?

Debs It's Boulogne. It's in France. Gordon's treating us to a little holiday in France.

Tony I don't wanna go to France. I want a compact disc player.

Debs It'll be nice. We'll get to go on a catamaran.

Tony A catamawhat?

Debs A big catamaran, a Supercat.

Tony Across the sea on a Supercat? What do we do, all hang on to its collar? Is there like a huge tin of Whiskas in France and we hang on and the cat goes meeaaaiiioww.

Debs It'll be educational.

Tony I don't wanna be educated. I get enough of that at school.

Debs It cost a lot of money.

Tony Well good, he can take the tickets back and buy me a compact disc player instead. And anyway, what's he doing forking out for a trip to France on the first date? It is the first date isn't it? You can't fool Inspector Morse! Lewis!

Josie Whyaye sir?

Tony I've got a job for you.

Josie Eeh, I was hoping to get home early sir, it's the wife's aerobics class.

Tony No such luck Lewis, now, give me nine pints of beer and a recording of the Brandenburg Concerto. When you've done that, arrest these two for seeing each other in stubterfuge. I mean in subterfudge. Seeing each other in slobterfidge. Have you two been seeing each other behind my back?

Debs I think I heard the doorbell, that must be Aunt Lucy. We'll have to go Gordon, we're late.

She exits

Tony circles Gordon like a jackal stalking an injured bird. Gordon looks distinctly uncomfortable

Tony You've been sneaking around haven't you, seeing my mother on the sly? Lying! Admit it! A typical grown-up trick! You're blushing! I knew it! Guilty!

Gordon is horrified

The set transforms into a courtroom. Household objects rise and form a dock around Gordon. Josie becomes the judge

Josie What is the charge?

Tony M'lady, that this man is a hardened criminal who thinks nothing of trifling with the affections of a young widow and attempting to ingratiate himself with her loving son by common or garden bribery. Has he uttered one word in his defence?

Gordon looks speechless

No! Has he said one word by way of explanation? No! I put it to you that the evidence he has given before this court is nothing more than a tissue of evasion and half truth. A web of deceit and slibbterfadge! In short, Rodney you plonker, a lorryload of porkies. (*He points off dramatically*)

A dog appears dressed as a policeman

Gordon is petrified

Josie Gordon Stanley Duffelcoat Sandalshoe Walker, you have been found guilty of being a lying grown-up. Do you admit the offence?

Gordon nods pitifully

It is my painful duty to pass sentence.

Gordon drops to his knees and begs for mercy. The sniggering dog drags him upright again

You will be taken from this court to the seaside and placed upon a Supercat which will then take off for a very bumpy ride across the water and you'll be joggled around until you're sick and you vomit everywhere ...

There is the sound of seagulls. The set transforms into a Supercat. Gordon looks queasy. A dog steps forward and commences (in mime) a safety drill demonstration. This includes swimming, screaming, and drowning

Tony (*to the audience*) Have you ever been on a Supercat? I mean they're massive.

Josie Hundreds of seats in rows and all these people ...

Tony And it can be really rough when the wind gets going, and the stewardesses point out all this stuff you have to do in case it sinks.

Josie Seems a bit daft to me.

Tony Why?

Josie I mean, you'll still be in the middle of the sea.

Tony So?

Josie You'd still drown, you'd just die standing up, at least if you stayed on board you could die sitting down.

Tony You're weird.

Josie And you're smelly.

Tony Anyway you're not even supposed to be in this part of the story. I haven't even met you yet.

Josie Right I'm going. (*To the audience*) Boys are so silly.

Tony (*to the audience*) Girls are so simple. Simple pimple. Pimple!

Josie Suffer.

Josie exits. Debs enters with a couple of drinks from the bar. Everyone sways with the motion of the crossing

Debs What are you saying about girls, Tony?

Tony Nothing Mum.

Debs (*handing him a drink*) There's yours.

Tony Thanks. Can I go on deck?

Debs It's too windy, you might get blown away.

Tony You still feeling queasy, Gordon?

Gordon nods

You've gone green. Don't worry, it'll only last another half an hour, then you can be in France and have lots of lovely French food, like snails and garlic.

Gordon throws up

Way to go Gordon. At this rate we'll soon have a bag each. (*He hands sick-bags to members of the audience; addressing them*) Here. Present for you. Don't worry, you'll all get one. Has anybody got a hat we can borrow? Or a duffel bag?

Gordon throws up again

You'd better get used to it folks! I mean we haven't had carrots since last
Tuesday. There's still four and a half days of dinner to come up yet!

Gordon staggers to his feet

Debs *(to Gordon)* Toilet?
Tony Oh dear, it's gonna be coming out of both ends is it?
Debs *(to Gordon)* Go on, love.
Tony Think about those sprouts we had on Sunday.
Debs I'll be with you in a minute.

Gordon exits

Tony So I'll just sit here on my own then?
Debs Don't go on love, please.
Tony *(to the audience)* Typical grown-up. When you want to watch the telly
or play games, they tell you to put them away and talk like a proper person.
But when you want to talk they say ...
Debs Just sit there and play quietly.

She exits

Tony I didn't mind. With Death-Dealer you've got to really concentrate. I
mean it's not chucking bricks like Super Mario, loading up some daft lorry,
and it's not just kung fu kicks and machine guns like some John Claude Van
Dumb film, it's complicated stuff. It's more complicated than maths! More
complicated than chemicals or hydrology, I'll bet! Before you know it the
game's over and you've arrived at the end. And before we knew it, we had!

*The set transforms into France. There are two basic sets now: a hotel room
with a balcony looking out to the moon and a café with a fruit stall next to it*

Gordon is in bed in the hotel room

France! You ever been there? Anybody ever been to France? I haven't, I
know I pretended that I didn't wanna come but that was just to get up
Gordon's nose. Really it's a bit of an adventure, I don't know what to
expect! Could be totally flat with no trees and no hills ... No, there's a hill,
there's a tree ... Could be bright green with yellow rivers. No, bricks are red,

roads are black ...

*A waiter enters and begins setting up a café table. He is a French half mask
dog. All the French dogs speak perfect French*

Perhaps it all looks OK on the surface but underneath it all the people are
turning into onions ... deedoodeedoodeedoo, the Twilight Zone. (*He
imitates Captain Kirk*) "Oh, Spock, what, are, we, doing, here, in, this,
God-forsaken, land ... it's so ... boring ... there's loads of people, shopping,
driving, riding their bikes ...with their little onion legs ..."

The waiter takes offence

Nothing personal ... As it happens it looks like anywhere else, shops, cafés,
boats, but all the names are different! *Boulangerie, pâtisserie* ... wow, those
cakes look fantastic! Gordon would like those, he's very fond of cream
cakes. How ya doing, Gordon?

Gordon sits up in bed, waves feebly and goes back to sleep

He's still a bit queasy. He's crashed out on the bed, ha ha, and that means
me and Mum can go out together.

Debs enters

Debs Tony, let's get something to eat!
Tony Great, food! Feed me! Feed me!

*The waiter hands Tony and Debs a menu. They each take a seat at the café
table*

Debs What do you fancy?
Tony What've they got?
Debs (*speaking fluent French*) *Bœuf Bourguignon, huîtres*, a selection of
    fromages——
Tony What's all that?
Debs French food.
Tony I don't want that muck! Why can't we have proper British food?
    Spaghetti? Or hamburgers? Or pizza or spring rolls or poppadoms?
Debs Well at least try something.
Tony Egg and chips.

Debs *Œuf pommes frites s'il vous plaît, garçon.*

The waiter writes down the order

Tony Oy mate, forget the erffing pom freets, just stick to the egg and chips.

The waiter exits

(*Standing up and shouting*) Gordon? Fancy a fried egg? You know, a half cooked one where the white of it's still a bit snotty? A lovely runny snotty egg? We could throw it up to you? And you could throw it up to us? Wimp! Wussy wimp!

Debs Leave him alone, he's still not well.

Tony How long have you known him then?

Debs About a year.

Tony A year! Why didn't you ever bring him home until now?

Debs You know why.

Tony What's that supposed to mean?

Debs You've never liked any of my boyfriends. You've always made it difficult for them.

Tony I haven't.

Debs You have, ever since ...

Tony Look at the shape of that man's hat!

Debs You know what I'm talking about. Ever since ...

Tony That car's a funny colour.

The waiter enters

Oh great, food. I love French food, I'm starving.

The waiter serves them their food, then exits

Egg and chips. Oh great.

Debs Darling, I'm trying to tell you something very important and you keep changing the subject.

Tony And that's when I saw Josie for the first time ever, right Mum! Look at that kid!

Debs Tony.

Tony This amazing weird kid.

Debs We brought you here for a reason, we thought——

Tony No I mean it. This incredible-looking kid.

Debs We thought it would be easier for you if we broke the news away from home because the thing about travel is that you get used to the idea of things being different, of things being changed. And nothing can stay the same you know. Things change. Things live, and grow and die.

Tony But Mum, Mum, look at the kid.

Debs Tony, I'm going to have a baby, a little brother or sister. And Gordon and me are going to get married when we get back to England. We think we'd like to.

Josie enters. She is pale, bald and heavily wrapped up

Tony Weird looking! Must be French, maybe all French people look like that, maybe all the rest have been tourists and she's the first French person we've seen. (*To Debs*) Have a baby?

Josie Who are you staring at?

Debs That's right.

Josie You staring at me?

Tony You and Gordon?

Josie You stare at me and I'll punch your teeth in.

Josie's mother (masked) appears, sees her runaway daughter and embraces her

Tony is fascinated and stares as Josie's mother attempts to make Josie wear a large woollen cap to hide her baldness. Debs smacks Tony's hand lightly and whispers to him under her breath, trying to get him to stop looking, but he is engrossed

Josie glowers at Tony, throws the cap to the floor and runs away. Her mother picks up the cap and runs after her

Debs That's right. Me and Gordon are going to——

Tony I heard. I wasn't trying to change the subject. It's like every time you want to talk about Dad dying, then you tell me I'm trying to change the subject.

Debs You always do try and change the subject.

Tony I wasn't trying to change the subject, I was just looking at the kid.

Debs I saw her.

Tony Weird looking. French.

Debs She isn't French, she's English.

Tony Funny voice.

Debs She's from the North.

Tony She's bald.

Debs She's ill. She's sick.

Tony Probably the food. These chips are disgusting!

Debs I wanted you to hear it from both of us, but I need to know what you think.

Tony I think I'm going to throw up.

Debs I think Gordon will make a very good father.

Tony You're making me sick. He makes me sick. I'm gonna be sick.

Debs We have to talk.

Tony I don't wanna talk. I don't wanna talk to anybody. I hate this place, I hate you and I hate your baby!

He runs off

Debs (*calling*) Tony——

The waiter enters

Oh, *pardonnez-moi monsieur* ... (*She clears the table with an embarrassed fluster and throws money at the waiter. Calling*) Tony, please.

Debs and the waiter exit

The stage once again takes on a nightmarish quality. A surreal washing line appears

Tony enters and hides behind the washing line. Josie enters and hides at the other end. They don't see each other

Tony I ran and I ran and I heard her calling me and shouting for the police but it didn't matter, there was no way I was going back to her.

Debs appears

Debs (*shouting*) Tony, where are you? I'm sorry, I love you, come back ... Come back love, please. Help! ... *Au secours* ... Police ... *Gendarme* ... Police? (*With a French accent*) Poleez?

She sees Josie, who wraps a sheet around her head to hide her baldness and pretends to be an old woman

Où la?

Josie La?

Debs *Où la?*
Josie La?
Debs *Où la la?* Damn ...

Debs runs off

Josie *(confronting Tony)* You!
Tony You!
Josie Come looking for a fight?
Tony Any time.
Josie Any time. But not just now.
Tony 'Cos I'm hiding.
Josie 'Cos I'm running away.

Josie exits and the washing line disappears. Tony hides under the table

Tony Suddenly the funny kid was gone and I couldn't see Mum and there was nobody, just France, just empty France. She's too old to have a baby. She can't even look after me, letting me run away and get lost and it's cold and it's starting to rain.

A forest of umbrellas appears

Leaving me alone to make my own way through French umbrellas ... 'Scuse me, 'scuse me! She's a terrible mother!

Debs runs on, flushed, panicking

Debs *(calling)* Tony, Tony! Where the hell are you? I'll strangle you when I get hold of you.

She exits

Tony You're a terrible mother! Babies, I hate them! What does she want to have a baby for?

He runs around the stage. Wherever he goes he is thwarted by images of the monstrous baby Josie; they pop out of flower pots, emerge from drainpipes, the cooker etc. Tony attempts to force them back into their hidey holes

Babies are horrible! A lot of my mates' mums and dads have had babies and they're really sneaky about it, what they say is, "It's going to be really good fun and you'll really love your little brother or sister", but what they mean is some fat bald monster is going to come into your house, take over the spare room, cover the floor with their toys, get all the attention and actually take over your life, actually! Attack!

A huge sumo wrestler-type baby Josie appears. Tony squares up to it with the full ritual of sprinkling salt, etc. Tony and the sumo baby wrestle

Josie enters, running away from her mother. The sumo baby bounces against Tony, who in turn collides with Josie

The baby exits

Josie Hide! Quick!
Tony Who you running away from?
Josie My mum.
Tony Me too.

They hide

Debs enters and frantically runs from one side of the stage to the other

Debs (*calling*) Tony, please, for God's sake, Tony ...

She exits

Josie takes a piece of paper from her pocket and begins to fold it

Josie Got a pen?
Tony Yeah. What you making?
Josie A chancer. (*She constructs it*) See, you fold it like this, then like this, then like this, right? So you have to write instructions on this bit, or fortune-telling things or whatever, and then colours here and numbers there.
Tony What are you making it for?
Josie Helps pass the time when you're hiding. You scared?
Tony No!
Josie I bet you are. I bet it's the first time you've run away. How old are you?
Tony Eight. Nearly.
Josie How old really?
Tony Seven and a bit. How old are you?
Josie Nine. You are scared aren't you? (*She finishes making the chancer*)

Tony I'm not. Can I have a go?
Josie All right, what's your name?
Tony Tony.
Josie (*with the chancer*) T.O.N.Y. Now choose a colour.
Tony Purple.
Josie P.U.R.P.L.E. Right now you've got to promise that whatever this says you'll do it.
Tony Promise.
Josie Or you'll die a horrible, painful, lingering death.
Tony Promise.
Josie Cross your heart.
Tony Cross my heart.
Josie Spit on your mother's life.
Tony Spit on me mother's life.
Josie Choose a number.
Tony Six.
Josie (*opening the chancer and reading*) It says "You must give Josie a kiss."
Tony What? No!
Josie Shhh.
Tony I'm not kissing you! Try another one.
Josie Well if you won't do this one than you really will die in agony. We'll use your full name this time. What is it?
Tony Tony Mason. Yellow. Number three.
Josie (*reading the chancer*) "Take down your trousers and show us your bum."
Tony No way!
Josie Come on, you've gotta do one of them.
Tony Well I'm definitely not showing you me bum!
Josie Well you'll have to kiss me then.
Tony Oh no. Oh this is horrible ... I wish I'd never heard of this stupid game.
Josie I'm waiting.
Tony Do I have to?
Josie Yes, after three. One. Two. Three.

She puckers up. He attempts to kiss her briefly but she grabs him by the neck and snogs him. He breaks free, mortified

Tony (*loudly*) Yeeeeeeuuuuuurrrrrrrrgggggggghhhhhh!
Josie Do you want another go?
Tony No I don't!
Josie Shhh. Somebody's coming.

Josie's mother and a Gendarme dog enter, cross the stage and exit

Josie and Tony hide

Tony Who's that?
Josie My mum.
Tony Who's that with her?
Josie *Gendarme*. French cop.
Tony Thought it might be your dad.
Josie No, my dad's back at the hotel. He had oysters last night. Been throwing up since three this morning. Projectile vomiting, real hughie.
Tony Yeah, Gordon did that last night. Red wine all over white walls. Looked like the revenge of Freddy Krueger.
Josie Well, little bit of sick never hurt anybody. Gordon your dad?
Tony No, he's my mum's boyfriend.

Gordon appears with a Gendarme. They rush across the stage and disappear in the wings, only to rush back again, seconds later. They exit during the following

That's him, gormless Gordon with the French copper. The John dim, or John don, or Jim Beam or whatever.
Josie *Gendarme.*
Tony You speak French then, do you?
Josie *Mais oui.*
Tony I said do you speak French then do you?
Josie *Mais oui* means yes.
Tony Oh, I didn't know. Why did you run away from your mum?
Josie I get sick of people staring at me like you did but when I say I'll smash them up mum gets really worried, then she starts to cry.
Tony Why?
Josie 'Cos she's a mum.

A Gendarme dog appears

Tony They've got the dogs on us now.
Josie They'll find us before long. They always do.

A Sniffer dog enters

The Sniffer dog spots Tony and Josie, and points them out to the Gendarme dog but the Gendarme dog doesn't notice

Sniffer dog (*to the Gendarme dog*) ICI! (*Here!*)
Gendarme dog (*on its own trail*) No, ici ici, Michel, ici, ici ...
Sniffer dog NO, HENRI, ICI!
Gendarme dog Ici, here. Ici!

The Gendarme dog exits

Sniffer dog Oh, sacré bleu ... Qu'est-que c'est le point? Henri est merde ...

The Sniffer dog disconsolately follows the Gendarme dog off

Tony So come on, tell me, why do you keep running away?
Josie It keeps them on their toes. I ran away at Euro-Disney. Dad got furious and ended up having a fight with Mickey Mouse. Oh Pluto. Oh Minnie, oh goddammm ...
Tony Euro-Disney? Your mum and dad must be rich.
Josie No. We just travel round so much now there's no time for him to do his job. Where do you live?
Tony London.
Josie I'm coming there in two weeks' time.
Tony Come and see me.
Josie I don't know where you live.
Tony I'll write it down.

Josie gives him the scrap of paper used to make the square for the chancer

Josie (*referring to the chancer*) You sure you don't want another go?
Tony No I don't. Here if you're bored, you can play with this. (*He hands her his Death-Dealer*)
Josie Death-Dealer level one hundred.
Tony Yeah, brand new, just out. I might be the first person in London to have one. First in England.
Josie I got mine three months ago.
Tony Three months? Was it your birthday?
Josie No. I just saw it in a shop and said I liked it and Dad bought it for me. Ever since I've had cancer they've given me everything I wanted.
Tony Colour telly?
Josie Yep.
Tony Portable compact disc player?
Josie Uh-huh.
Tony Good Swatch?

Josie (*showing it to him*) The best.

Tony Huh, I wish I had cancer.

Josie They thought I'd beaten it but I've got another tumour.

Tony Is that one of them things they play in the orchestra?

Josie No that's a tuba. This is a tumour.

Tony Can I have a look? Is it like a big pussy boil? Has it got a scab on it? When nobody's looking in the middle of the night do you pick the scab off and eat it?

Josie No, it's inside.

Tony Inside? That's no fun.

Josie No, it isn't. How far have you got?

Tony Level thirty-seven. It's a tough one this one isn't it?

Josie My doctor keeps telling me she's got to level sixty but I don't believe her.

Tony Your doctor plays Death-Dealer? Good doctor.

Josie She reckons that when you start off it seems impossible but you just have to do little victories, take things in stages, one step at a time. Right, I'm gonna go back to my hotel, they'll have worried enough by now. Thanks for the address.

They emerge from their hiding place

Josie's mother enters from one side of the stage and Gordon enters from the other. They see their respective children and rush forward to embrace them. Josie's mother takes Josie off stage

Tony steps out of Gordon's embrace

Tony (*addressing the audience*) When Gordon found me I half expected him to try and clip me round the ear but he didn't. He just looked sad and hurt. He wasn't even angry. But Mum was!

They return to the hotel room. Debs is in a furious temper and throws clothes, etc., at Tony and Gordon, expecting them to pack. Tony is alarmed at her ferocity. Gordon starts to pack

Debs I must be mad thinking this would work, I mean I've tried and it's tough you know bringing up a kid on your own! I was twenty-two when your dad died, they wanted to take you into care, said I couldn't cope but I said "Not on your life, he's my boy and I'm keeping him." Gordon, can't you even fold up a jumper properly!

She tips the contents of the case which Gordon has been trying to pack on to the floor. He sighs hugely, goes to embrace and comfort her, decides against it and begins repacking the case

But make no mistake it's no bloody picnic, never having a night off and never having enough money and never being able to see anybody properly because my son is a selfish little monster and then when I do find a bloke I like, all right he's not exactly Superman, I mean he wears sandals and a duffel coat for God's sake, I mean he needs a lot of work but underneath it all he's basically kind and caring, he turns out to be the kind of wimp who throws up every five minutes and takes two and a half hours to find a runaway kid and I miss your dad!

The fury evaporates and she is left in tears. Gordon gently approaches her and strokes her hair. Tony watches in shocked silence. Eventually Debs and Gordon kiss. Then Gordon calmly ushers Tony out of the room. Tony watches as Gordon goes back into the room, cuddles Debs and switches off the light

The hotel room disappears

Tony goes up on the balcony above the hotel room and stares at the moon and the café below

Tony After she had started to cry Gordon gave her a cuddle and I went out. I thought it might be nice for them to be alone.

Below, outside the café, a French dog enters and begins to play a melancholy tune on an accordion

The air was fresh and I could hear music and laughter from the café downstairs ... And suddenly it all seemed right, like things had changed and things were different but somehow I'd changed as well. I couldn't work out what it was but I thought it probably had something to do with Josie. And Death-Dealer. And my dad.

Two other dogs enter. One is a female torch singer

The three dogs begin playing boule, a magical game in which the balls make patterns in the air before landing

And all of a sudden for the first time in ages I got this big lump in my throat and it felt like a cricket ball, it was so big and my eyes felt as wide as moons

and without any warning these big hot tears came out, big wet hot tears
running down my cheeks like a bathroom tap, and although I didn't make
any noise, inside I howled like a dog in the night, and thought about going
home.

*The dogs notice Tony's tears, and abandon their game to comfort him with
a song*

Dogs (*singing*)   Life
Is a gay
Cabaret
Mon ami
But there's no
Guarantee
Of applause
OK
So you play
By the rules
Mon ami
But it's not quite as simple as boules
Mon ami
For fortune makes dogs into fools
Mon ami
And 'appiness slips through
Ze paws
But if
You can smile
Through the tears
Mon amis
Le petit
Victory
Will be yours.

Black-out

CURTAIN

ACT II

The kitchen set. Six months later

Josie is trying to reason with Tony, who is engrossed in Death-Dealer

Tony (*to the audience*) And when I got up next morning, Josie and her mum and dad had gone. (*To Josie*) Hadn't you?

Josie It wasn't my fault, we got up really early, and I didn't get a chance to say goodbye to you.

Tony Things were different when we got back home. Gordon and Mum were getting on really well and for the first time in years she seemed happy. I waited ages and ages for you to get in touch, but you didn't!

Josie I was ill!

Tony You could easily have written to me!

Josie I got very sick!

Tony I gave you my address!

Josie It wasn't my fault.

Tony Not listening. Go away. I am playing Death-Dealer, I can't hear you.

Josie I couldn't help it, Tony, honestly. I wanted to talk to you but I got really sick, and sometimes when I'm sick I don't know what's happening, or I forget things, or it's just like I'm asleep most of the time!

Tony I'm not listening.

Josie Please, Tony, please listen to me.

Tony You should have called me.

Josie I would have done but I couldn't. I wanted to, I missed you. I thought about you.

Tony Did you?

Josie Yes. I thought about you a lot.

Tony I thought about you. Every time I played Death-Dealer.

Josie It's a good game.

Tony It's even better when you play it with a friend.

Josie Are you ready to play?

Tony Yo!

Josie Are we going to lose?

Tony No!

Josie So stand by your console! Let's go!

Tony Go, go, go! Let's play Death-Dealer!

Josie A story of birth!

Tony And death!

Josie⎫
Tony⎬ (*together*) And the bit in between.

Tony (*declaiming*) WITH A SWORD CALLED PEACE AND A STAFF CALLED TRUTH WE'LL FACE THE STERNEST TASK, SO DEBONAIR AND DEVIL MAY CARE——

Josie —AS HE WEARS THE HERO'S MASK——

Tony —IF THEY ASK——

Josie —WHO IS THAT STURDY MAN——

Tony —HAS HE GOT——

Josie —WHAT IT TAKES——

Tony —TO PLOT AND PLAN——

Josie —CAN HE WIN?——

Tony —THEN I'LL GRIN OF COURSE I CAN——

Josie —OF COURSE I CAN——

Josie⎫
Tony⎬ (*together*)   OF COURSE I CAN.
                              THE FOOT OF THE MOUNTAIN
                              THE SHORE OF THE SEA
                              THE PATH TO THE FOREST
                              THE ROOT OF THE TREE
                              THE SILENT WIZARD
                              THE DOOR AND ITS KEY
                              THE EDGE OF ADVENTURE
                              IS BECKONING ME
                              THE EDGE OF ADVENTURE
                              IS BECKONING ME.

Tony The first thing we have to do is work out which level we're at.

Josie Level eighty-three. Now the object of the game is to find out what is in the Basket of Light——

They pull things from out under the sink and act out the game using various props. Celery for the forest, a pan scrubber for the witch, etc.

——but to get to the Basket of Light you have to go through this huge maze ...

Tony And escape from the witch——

Josie —and go deep into the forest——

Tony —then get past the geysers of stone ... into the enchanted fortress——

Josie —facing up to Skullmort the Reaper——

Tony — dodging him and his dragons——

Josie —snatching the Basket of Light out of his hands——

Tony —and then, bring it all the way past Skullmort and his dragons out of the fortress, through the forest, past the geysers of stone and the mirror of the past, out to the threshold, avoiding the poison berries, back on the magic carpet across the stormy sea, back to the mainland and handing over the basket to the Queen, right?

Josie Right!

Tony I'd have liked to have played it with you.

Josie Yeah. So would I.

For a moment it seems as if they might hold hands, but they don't

Josie exits

Tony We never did get a chance to play the game together. 'Cos like I said I never heard from her. I just played it by myself when I got back from France. I played it while Mum and Gordon planned their wedding. I played it during the wedding. I played it all through the honeymoon when they went to Edinburgh and I had to stay with Aunty Lucy. I played it loads and loads and loads of times by myself. And then one night I was in my room and I had just got to an exciting bit when suddenly I heard Mum's voice and she said——

Debs (*off*) Tony!

Tony (*to the audience*) Mum.

Debs Come on, it's tea time.

Tony (*calling off to Debs*) Just five more minutes.

Debs appears at the door. She is heavily pregnant. During the following Gordon enters and starts cooking in the kitchen

Debs Come on love, your tea's ready.

Tony You OK?

Debs Just tired. Your baby brother or sister is obviously going to be a footballer when they grow up.

Tony What do you mean?

Debs Kicking.

Tony (*listening to the baby*) Weird! You can feel it. (*To the audience*) Do you want a go? You do, don't you? Mum, can my friends feel it kicking?

Debs Well, how many of them are there?

Tony About—(*counts the audience*) a million?

Debs No, Tony, I don't mind one or two but I draw the line at a million.

Tony Grown-ups eh? No fun. What's for tea?

Debs It's a surprise.

Things are not going terribly well in the kitchen. Smoke is coming out of various pots and pans. Eventually, Gordon serves up one portion of sludge

Tony What is it?
Debs Guess.
Tony Even somebody on *Mastermind* couldn't guess what that is. Or *Masterchef* (*mimicking Loyd Grossman*) "And what can we see through the keyhole this week?" A plate of gunge. Looks like the stuff Noël Edmonds dumps on people's heads. Gunge tank, gunge tank!
Debs Eat it up.
Tony It's gunge isn't it. I mean it's just gunge.
Debs I'm sure it's fine.
Tony Then why aren't you eating it?
Debs I'm not feeling hungry.
Tony Gordon?

Gordon shakes his head

   So you're not hungry either?

Gordon shakes his head

   Brilliant, so I'm the lucky lad who gets to eat all the grey gunge as served up by Gordon the sludge beast. Gordon the slop monster.

The telephone rings

Debs I'll get it. (*She picks up the telephone*)
Tony I pity the poor baby born into this house! Forced to eat this muck!
Debs (*speaking into the telephone*) Yes, speaking.
Tony I think it's my duty to warn it! All right so it's inside Mum but that means it's only like, four feet away. It might not be able to see but it must be able to hear what I'm saying.
Debs Yes, I have a son called Tony. What's he done?
Tony (*directing his whisper at Debs's stomach*) Hallo baby? Can you hear me baby?

The sumo baby Josie emerges from somewhere on the set

   (*To the sumo baby Josie*) Can you hear what I'm saying?

The baby Josie nods. Throughout the following scene it investigates the kitchen with all the curiosity of the newborn, switching things on, picking things up, etc. Debs and Gordon remain oblivious. Tony clears up any mess the baby makes

That's your mum right? You're inside her right now. This is you here.

He pats Debs's bulge. She remains unaware

Of course being inside you'll never have seen her before. I'll bet you thought she was really glamorous, eh? Well tough, no, that's our mum and we're stuck with her. And this over here is your dad, Gordon. See the resemblance?

The baby is dismayed at the thought that Gordon is its father

So do you reckon you're daddy's boy or girl? What are you anyway?

The baby turns its back to the audience and checks its nappy. But it doesn't know whether it's a boy or a girl

Well whatever you are you're gonna have to eat the rubbish he's cooked.
Debs Who? Josie who? Boulogne?
Tony Boulogne? Is that Josie on the phone?
Debs It's Josie's mum. Eat your supper, Tony, like a good lad.
Tony (*to the baby*) I mean try it.

The baby tries the food and doesn't like it

You think that's bad. Wait 'til you see what we had yesterday.

He opens the fridge and takes out two bowls of differently coloured gunge

That's supposed to be stew, this one's lasagne and that's ratatouille made with real rats. All disgusting. Couldn't taste any worse if you mixed them all together.

The baby does just this

Debs Gordon, pass me a pencil would you?

Gordon gets up and gives Debs a pencil. The baby makes a huge mess on the table

Tony Look at all this mess. I'll get the blame for this. (*He places the plate full of multi-coloured gunge on one corner of the table and attempts to clean up*)
Debs Ward Twelve. Yes, I'll tell him. Yes, I know where it is.

Gordon goes to lean on the table, inadvertently heading straight for the plate of gunge

Tony (*distracting Gordon*) A wasp! (*He shifts the plate to Gordon's chair*)

Gordon looks around in horror but can find no wasp. He relaxes and leans against the table

Sorry, could've sworn I saw a wasp. (*To the baby*) You nearly got me into trouble there. Go on, go back to your womb and stay there.

The baby disappears

Debs Yes, I'll ask him, but you do understand—... Yes quite... All right then, bye.

She replaces the telephone

That was Josie's mum, remember, the little girl in France. Josie's very ill, she's in hospital and she'd like to see you but it could be a bit distressing. She's dying, Tony. She hasn't got long left. Do you want to go and see her?
Tony Sure.
Debs (*upset*) Gordon will take you. I'll just get a hankie.

She exits

Tony Of course I'll go and see her. Just wish it wasn't in hospital that's all. I hate hospitals. I mean the one Dad was in was all right and the people were great but there was nothing they could do. See, the thing is, sometimes there isn't. But yeah, I'll go and see her. But don't you trouble yourself, Gordon.

Gordon is surprised by his friendliness

You've done an awful lot today. Washed, scrubbed and cooked this lovely supper, you must be exhausted.

Gordon nods appreciatively

You just sit down and take it easy. (*He takes Gordon by the shoulders and sits him down on the plate of gunge*) There. That's better isn't it?

The set transforms into a hospital room. There is a telephone next to Josie's bed

Gordon and Tony exit

Josie is in bed playing Death-Dealer with her doctor. Josie looks smaller, iller, thinner. The doctor is a full mask character

Josie Are you going to do the operation yourself?

The doctor nods

If it goes wrong will you promise me something?

The doctor nods

(*She whispers in the doctor's ear*) Promise?

The doctor nods and whispers a question into Josie's ear

No he is not my boyfriend! Cheeky rat!

Tony and Gordon enter. Tony has a bunch of flowers

Tony God, I hate the smell of hospitals ...

The doctor ushers Gordon and Tony in. Gordon hangs back while Tony approaches the bed. He and Josie are rather shy in each other's presence

Tony Hi.
Josie Hi.
Tony Flowers.
Josie Nice.
Tony For you.
Josie Ta.

Tony But don't get the wrong idea. It's not like I'm your boyfriend or
anything.
Josie No. Can you put these in some water please, Doctor? And stop
laughing!

The doctor takes the flowers and exits

Tony How you doing?
Josie All right.
Tony Right.
Josie How you doing?
Tony All right.
Josie Right.
Tony You look thinner.
Josie You look fatter.
Tony You look balder.
Josie You look hairier. Hi Gordon.
Tony Say Hi, Gordon!

Gordon waves shyly

Tony He's shy. He's a wally.
Josie He's nice. You're nice, Gordon.

Gordon is pleased

Take your duffel off.

*Gordon removes his duffel and looks for somewhere to hang it. He almost
hangs it on Josie's drip feeder but realizes that might be a mistake*

Tony He must really like you. He hardly ever takes his duffel off in public.
I'm begining to think he's not a man at all, he's Paddington Bear trying to
live quietly under an assumed name.
Josie Has he married your mum yet?
Tony Yeah. Ages ago.
Josie Good wedding?
Tony No.
Josie Why not?
Tony I had to wear a suit.
Josie Ha ha! I bet you looked like a monkey!
Tony No I didn't.

Gordon nods

Well actually, yes I did.
Josie Has she had the baby yet?
Tony Any minute now.
Josie You excited, Gordon?

Gordon gives a bad impression of someone with nerves of steel

Boy or girl?
Tony Don't know.
Josie They can tell. Scans.
Tony She doesn't want to know. Won't have one. She's had lots of rows with the doctors. So. Why didn't you come and see me after Boulogne?
Josie Regression.
Tony What does that mean?
Josie I got worse.
Tony How bad?
Josie They're going to operate. Find out. But it looks bad.
Tony Are you going to die?

Gordon is alarmed by this but Josie is calm

Josie I might, I might not. Who knows? I'll fight. I might win, I might lose.
Tony What —what happens when you die?
Josie Good question. I don't know.
Tony When my dad died—
Josie Yeah?
Tony I think he turned into a bell. On the moon. But a really high-pitched bell, so high nobody but dogs can hear it.
Josie A bell?
Tony A bell.
Josie Do you think it's true?
Tony It's true if I believe it.
Josie Do you believe it?
Tony I don't know. (*To the audience*) And then something really strange happened.
Josie A bell. I like that. I like the sound of a bell.

A telephone rings. The noise startles Gordon

Tony Gordon, the phone's ringing.

The coincidence has frightened Gordon

Come on, get it together! Answer the phone!

Eventually Gordon answers the telephone. He does not react at first but then he panics and puts the phone down, stunned

Mum?

Gordon nods

Josie The baby?

Gordon nods

You're going to be a daddy!

Gordon nods

Tony Well don't just stand there, go!

Gordon runs off. Then he runs back on to look for his duffel, bumping into things as he does so. Eventually, after a tussle, he finds the coat, and runs off

Josie and Tony are left alone. There is an awkward silence

Josie I cracked Death-Dealer.
Tony You've done it?
Josie Once.
Tony Once is enough! Well wicked! So you've actually looked into the Basket of Light?
Josie Maybe.
Tony And you know what's in there?
Josie Might do.
Tony So are you going to tell me what it is?
Josie Possibly.
Tony When?
Josie After the operation.

The doctor enters

Oh oh. Time to go. I know the drill, don't worry.

The doctor removes the drip from Josie's arm

I'm scared.
Tony Eh.
Josie I'm scared, Tony.
Tony Nothing to be scared of, right.
Josie It's an adventure, right?
Tony Right. Just ... it's the beginning of the game, right. On to the magic carpet.
Josie Goodbye, Tony.
Tony See you later.
Josie Maybe.

The doctor wheels Josie off. Tony is left alone

Tony I just wait here, do I? I said I just wait here. Do I? Hallo? What do I do? What do I do? (*To the audience*) There was only one thing I could do. (*He picks up Death-Dealer*) One last try, Death-Dealer. Level one hundred!

The set transforms into the Death-Dealer landscape. A heart monitor effect gives us an eerie percussion. A giant projection shows us Josie's heartbeat

Here we stand on the threshold of the forest. (*He calls*) Josie, Josie, where are you?

Josie appears

Are you ready to play?
Josie Yo.
Tony Are you going to lose?
Josie No.
Tony }
Josie } (*together*) Let's go.
Tony First we just stare into the mirror and learn the truth of the past.
Josie Right, the truth is this, your dad died aged thirty-one, these things happen, life goes on.
Tony And so does death! Next step?

Josie Escaping from the witch, easy, jump three steps——

They do

——and then produce the sword called "Peace" and the staff called "Truth".

The sword and staff appear magically

Tony Then enter the forest to face Skullmort the Reaper.
Josie But beware. The forest floor contains ten geysers which will turn you to stone if you step upon them. Right, let's see who goes first. (*She uses the chancer to decide*) Your full name this time.
Tony T.O.N.Y. M.A.S.O.N.
Josie Oh oh. It says I'm first.
Tony Test the way with the staff of truth ... see and be careful!

He reaches out with the staff and touches the floor. A geyser of steam shoots up into the air

Josie Wish me luck.
Tony You'll need it!

Josie crosses the geyser field, obeying Tony's instructions as he plays the game

Tony Right ... left ... careful ... left ...

Josie feels her way with the staff. The geysers explode all around her but she reaches the next section unharmed. A figure (Skullmort the Reaper) begins to grow. A bridge forms between Josie and him. As the tension mounts the beat of the heart monitor quickens. Eventually Josie traverses the floor and successfully reaches the bridge

She's done it. Hooray!
Josie I am here, I am ready. Where is Skullmort the Reaper?

Skullmort appears. He is huge and threatening

Tony Go on go on. What are you waiting for? Kill him!
Josie I can't.
Tony Why not?
Josie I'm not strong enough. I just have to face him as best I can. I can spit,

I can scream, I can cry, but I can't change it.

Tony But how are you going to get the basket?

Josie I'll have to take my chances ...

She crosses the bridge and is absorbed by Skullmort and his darkness. Then from within him comes a powerful light. We see her clasping a basket in her arms. Tony is screaming at her to leave but she is enthralled. The light grows mighty and Skullmort recedes. Now, she is ablaze with whiteness

Tony Josie!

He tries to cross but the geysers stop him

Josie! Don't die!

Then, suddenly, Josie is gone. The heart monitor effect is stilled and the set reforms into Tony's house. Tony is alone in half light

You can't die! You can't leave me! It's a terrible feeling to be left behind, like when Dad died, it's like being abandoned. What about me? What about me? No, it's not fair, it's not fair! What about me? (*He falls to his knees exhausted, crying*)

Debs enters

Debs Hey, hey, hey ...

Tony The game isn't fair. (*He throws Death-Dealer away*)

Debs Life never is. Or death.

Tony I don't want to play anymore.

Debs You will. There's so much to do. You have to help. It's not just me and you and Gordon now.

Tony Why did she have to die?

Debs We all have to die. But life goes on. And she left you a present.

Tony What present?

Debs Josie told the doctor how the game ends. She wanted you to know. Look ...

Gordon enters carrying a basket. Light comes from it

Tony The Silent Wizard. It all makes sense. The Silent Wizard rescues the basket? Right?

Gordon nods

And the hero opens the basket to find what's inside. Right? (*He takes the basket from Gordon*)

Gordon exits

Debs Right.
Tony And we all want to know what's inside the basket, right? Well the answer is——

The baby appears

——a baby. Josie two. Josie the sequel. Which is where the story started. Say hallo everybody. Say hallo, Josie.

The baby throws up

Charming. Well, little bit of sick——
Debs Never hurt anyone. And she is a bit excited.
Tony Well she would be. It is a special day.

Debs takes the baby

Gordon enters with a birthday cake, lit with one candle

Now. Everyone sing very quietly.

He leads the audience in singing happy birthday to Josie. She blows the candle out. Tony gives her three cheers

One year old.
Debs One year to the day since Josie died.
Tony A life taken.
Debs A life given.
Tony A new life for me and Mum and stupid old gormless Gordon.

Gordon looks sad and goes to exit

Except Gordon turned out to be anything but gormless.

Gordon stops in his tracks

Because he loves my mum and Josie and in a certain way, a sneaky sort of way, a sneaky grown-up sort of way he loves me. And in a sort of way, a sneaky sort of way... I love him.

He cuddles Gordon, who is stunned but delighted and cuddles him back

Gordon and Debs exit with baby Josie

I even put up with the latest present he bought me. You're not gonna believe this. (*He whistles*)

A dog appears and leaps on him, humping his leg

A dog for me to look after. Well, what with feeding it and taking it for a walk and trying to stop it spending its whole life sniffing other dogs' bums then licking me on the lips, it's a full-time job. And then of course looking after baby Josie and Mum and keeping Gordon out of trouble, you can see I've got my hands full.

He throws a bone for his dog. It barks

The pack of dogs enters

That's it ... fetch. Fetch. Good dogs!

They chase each other around before coming to rest at Tony's feet in a pile

By the end of the day I'm absolutely exhausted. I get into bed and Gordon reads me stories before I go to sleep, of dragons and monsters and heroes and death and life. And I drift off thinking big thoughts, important grown-up thoughts, knowing that however long we get a chance to live it, life is wonderful. Tonight, when you're in bed, think about that. But just before you drift off, when you're on the edge of sleep, just do me one last favour. Smile, think about the moon ... and listen.

Tony and the dogs howl at the moon. The moon responds with the sound of bells. Tinkling at first, then more clamorous, until the night is alive with their chimes

Black-out

CURTAIN

FURNITURE AND PROPERTIES

Only essential properties, furniture, etc. are listed here, as mentioned in the text.
Further dressing can be added at the director's discretion

ACT I

On stage: Cupboards
Sink
Fridge
Table
Chairs
Window blind
Microwave, washing machine, cooker, etc.
Flowerpots, drainpipes, etc.
Talc, cream, clean nappy, etc. **(Tony)**
Walkman **(Tony)**
Sick-bags (on Supercat) **(Tony)**
Suitcase, clothes (in hotel room, France) **(Debs)**
Telephone

Off stage: Eight carrier bags stuffed with food and nappies **(Deb)**
Dressing-gown **(Debs)**
Duffel coat **(Gordon)**
Present (wrapped Death-Dealer) **(Gordon)**
Envelope with tickets **(Gordon)**
Drinks **(Debs)**
Café table, menus **(French waiter)**
Food **(French waiter)**
Woollen cap **(Josie's mother)**
Sheet, scarf, etc. **(Josie)**
Accordion **(Dog)**
Balls for boule **(Dogs)**
Supercat (France)
Bed (hotel room, France)
Fruit stall (café, France)

Personal: **Tony**: baby Josie puppet with nappy, pen
       Debs: mac, money
       French waiter: pad, pen
       Josie: paper for chancer, Swatch watch

ACT II

Strike: French furniture and properties

Set: Kitchen set
       Under sink: Celery, pan scrubber, etc.
       Cooking implements: pots, pans, portions of gunge, etc.
       In fridge: Two portions of multi-coloured gunge
       Pencil (**Gordon**)
       Baby Josie puppet with nappy (**Tony**)
       Bone (**Tony**)

Off stage: Bed (hospital room, **Josie**)
       Drip feeder (hospital room, **Josie**)
       Telephone (hospital room)
       Flowers (**Tony**)
       Duffel coat (**Gordon**)
       Sword and Staff
       Basket (**Skullmort/Josie**)
       Basket with baby Josie puppet (**Gordon**)
       Birthday cake with one candle (**Gordon**)

Personal: **Tony**: Death-Dealer

LIGHTING PLOT

Only essential lighting plots are listed here. The lighting effects for the Death-Dealer sequences are left to the director's discretion

Practical fittings required: Light from Death-Dealer
                               Light in basket for Death-Dealer sequence

ACT I

To open: Stage in darkness. Luminous moon effect.

Cue 1	**Dogs** howl at the moon for the second time *Snap lights up on Tony and Josie*	(Page 1)
Cue 2	**Josie**: "Well unwrap it then." *Lightning effects*	(Page 8)
Cue 3	**Josie**: "I'm scared." *Death-Dealer landscape effects*	(Page 8)
Cue 4	**Josie**: "Oh, is that all." *Death-Dealer effects cease*	(Page 9)
Cue 5	**Tony**: "And before we knew it, we had." *Moon effect (until end of Act I)*	(Page 13)
Cue 6	**Debs**: "Tony, please." *Nightmare effects*	(Page 17)
Cue 7	**Tony**: "But Mum was!" *All effects cease (switch to hotel room lighting)*	(Page 23)
Cue 8	**Gordon** cuddles **Deb** and switches off light *Hotel room lighting off*	(Page 24)
Cue 9	**Dogs** (*singing*): "Ze paws." *Black-out*	(Page 25)

ACT II

To open: Kitchen lighting

Cue 10	**Tony: "Death-Dealer. Level one hundred!"** *Death-Dealer effect; projection of Josie's heartbeat, etc.*	(Page 36)
Cue 11	**Josie: "I'll have to take my chances ..."** *Light effects from Skullmort and Josie*	(Page 38)
Cue 12	**Tony: "Josie! Don't die!** *Death-Dealer effects cease. Tony is left in half light*	(Page 38)
Cue 13	**Tony: " Smile, think about the moon ..."** *Moon effect*	(Page 40)
Cue 14	**The bells get louder** *Black-out*	(Page 40)

EFFECTS PLOT

Only essential effects are listed here. The effects for the Death-Dealer sequences are left to the director's discretion. Many of them can be physically performed by the cast.

ACT I

Cue 1	Tony: " ... knew he was a plonker." *Barking sounds*	(Page 6)
Cue 2	Josie: "Well unwrap it then." *Thunder. Death-Dealer effects; rumbles, etc.*	(Page 8)
Cue 3	Josie: "I'm scared." *Further Death-Dealer effects. Images of baby Josie appear*	(Page 8)
Cue 4	Josie: "Look at Gordon!" *Magnets on the fridge move magically to spell* LIFE AND DEATH	(Page 8)
Cue 5	Josie: "Oh, is that all." *All effects cease*	(Page 9)
Cue 6	Tony: "I knew it! Guilty!" *Household objects rise to form courtroom*	(Page 11)
Cue 7	Tony: " ... and you vomit everywhere ..." *Sound of seagulls*	(Page 11)
Cue 8	Debs: "Tony, please." *Nightmare effects*	(Page 17)
Cue 9	Tony: " What does she want to have a baby for?" *Images of the baby appear*	(Page 18)

ACT II